The

Written by Roger Carr
Illustrated by Peter Paul Bajer

™ sundance

A Haights Cross Communications ®️ Company

"A fox! A fox!" Adam shouted.
"Dad! ...Mom! ...Dad! ...Mom!"
He ran from the pond to the farmhouse.

"A fox chased away the mother duck,
and he got all the ducklings!"

"Not all of them," Dad said. "Look!"
He pointed to the ground.
A little duckling was sitting on the grass,
looking up at Adam.

"One duckling is still here," Dad said.

Adam picked up the duckling.

He carried it back to the pond
and put it in the water.

"Swim out to the island," Adam said.
"There's a duck out there.
She'll look after you,
and the fox won't get you."

They all walked back to the house.
They had just gone inside
when Adam heard a noise at the door.

"Peep! Peep!"

"Hey! Dad! Mom! The duckling is back!
Why is it following me?" asked Adam.

"It thinks you are its mother," his Dad said.
"A duckling always thinks
the first moving thing it sees
is its mother."

"But I'm not its mother!" Adam said.

"The duckling thinks you are," Mom said.
"You'll have to take care of it now."

That afternoon,
Adam worked in the garden.
The duckling helped.
It ate the snails and the worms.

When it was bath time,
Adam got out his old baby tub.
He filled the tub with cold water
and put his old rubber duck in it.
Then he put the duckling in the tub.

Adam had a bath in warm, soapy water.

That night, Adam put a box in the laundry room for the duckling to sleep in. He hoped it would not be lonely.

"Peep! Peep!" said the duckling.

"You'll be all right," said Adam.

Adam was nearly asleep when he heard
"Peep! Peep!"
The duckling was standing beside
Adam's bed.

"Peep! Peep! Peep!" said the duckling
and hopped into one of Adam's shoes.

"Good night," said Adam.

The next morning, Adam fed the duckling.
Then he went to school.

14

"I've got a duckling for a pet,"
Adam told his friend Sam.

"I know," Sam said. "It's really cute."
"How do you know?" asked Adam.
Then he saw his bag.

"Oh no!" said Adam. "What will I do?"

"Bring him to Show and Tell," said Sam.

15

Everyone loved Adam's duckling.
The whole class wrote a poem.

Adam has a little duck.
It followed him to school.
And everyone in Adam's class
thinks the duck is really cool.